WILD GAME GOURMET: COOKING CRITTERS FOR DINNER

Refined Road Kill Recipes

Danny Gansneder

First Printing: 2015

ISBN-13: 978-1519793867
ISBN-10: 1519793863

CONTENTS

Photo by Olin Gilbert / CC BY 2.0

Wild game and outdoor cooking make the perfect fit. The methods that are best for cooking game outdoors are grilling, smoking, Dutch oven, and open fire camp cooking. It is important, however, not to minimize any safe food handling practices. Keeping meat at less than 40 degrees before cooking, cooking meat to the proper temperature, and maintaining clean work areas is essential to prevent spoilage and contamination.

But first, here's a good trick to get the wild taste out of the game meats like venison or elk. You can soak the meat with some beer, pineapple juice, Coke, or red wine. You will find that not only does it get out most of the game taste, but also adds a delicious flavor to the meat. And nothing goes better with eating all natural healthy wild game than using all natural and organic vegetables grown from only the best heirloom seed varieties.

These outdoor wild game recipes will show you how to cook wild game ranging from venison to dove, as well as several others. Wild game cooked outdoors opens up a whole different area of cooking with many delicious possibilities.

Photo by Matt Biddulph / CC BY-SA 2.0

- 4-6 1/2-inch Venison Steaks
- 1/4 cup Worcestershire sauce
- 1/4 cup your favorite BBQ sauce
- 1/4 cup steak sauce
- Salt
- Pepper

Mix the three sauces together. Add the salt and the pepper to taste and marinade the venison steaks for at least an hour before cooking. Cook the steaks on the grill over a medium-hot fire for about 5 minutes on each side.

Venison Steak Sauce

- 1/4 cup ketchup

- 1 tablespoon Worcestershire sauce
- 1/4 teaspoon garlic powder
- 1/4 teaspoon salt

Mix all the ingredients together.

GRILLED VENISON TENDERLOIN

- 8 slices bacon
- Venison tenderloin cut into 1-inch steaks
- 1/4 cup teriyaki sauce

Marinate the tenderloins in the teriyaki sauce for at least 4 hours. Then wrap each steak around the edge with a slice of bacon. Secure the bacon in place with a toothpick. Cook the meat over a charcoal fire for about 30 minutes.

Photo by *Everett Harper* / *CC BY-SA- 2.0*

- 2 ducks
- 1 tablespoon seasoning salt
- 1 fresh twigs of rosemary and thyme

First split the duck along the backbone and then mash the breastbone until the duck lies flat.
Slide the fresh rosemary and the thyme under the skin of the breasts and the legs. Sprinkle both sides of the duck with the seasoning salt.

Over a charcoal grill, with skin down, cook the bird until it has a nice brown color. Then turn the duck over and grill the other side until the meat is done.

GRILLED WILD DUCK FILETS

- 8 duck breast filets
- 2 large cloves of garlic finely minced
- 2 tablespoons minced fresh rosemary leaves
- 1 tablespoon minced fresh thyme
- Fresh ground black pepper

First soak the duck breasts overnight in a brine solution of one cup salt for every eight cups of water. Then remove the breasts from the brine and rinse. Add the fresh black pepper to the duck breasts and rub the spices thoroughly on the breasts and let the duck sit for an hour.

Grill the duck over medium heat until it reaches the desired doneness. Slice the duck breasts into thin slices across the grain and serve with some rice.

BARBEQUED QUAIL

- 6 semi boneless quail, rib cages removed and wing tips cut off
- 1 cup minced onion
- 1 cup white wine
- 1/4 cup honey
- 2 tablespoons Worcestershire sauce
- 4 large cloves of garlic, minced
- 1 tablespoon dry mustard
- 2 teaspoons Chile powder
- Salt

- Fresh ground black pepper

Combine all of the ingredients except the quail in a pan over the fire and let this simmer for 15 minutes. Remove the pan from the heat and let it cool.

Put the quail in a dish and pour about 2/3 of the marinade over the bird and marinate for an hour. Grill the quail for 4 minutes on each side. Using the marinade, baste the meat while cooking.

RUBY RED QUAIL

- 8 semi boneless quail
- Juice of 1 lemon
- 1/2 cup ruby red grapefruit juice
- 2 garlic cloves, crushed
- 2 tablespoons molasses
- 2 bay leaves
- 1 teaspoon dried thyme, crumbled
- 1 teaspoon dried hot red pepper flakes

In a bowl, mix together the grapefruit juice, the lemon juice, the garlic cloves, the bay leaves, the thyme, the molasses, and the red pepper flakes to make a marinade. Add the quail to this mixture, cover and let marinate for 4 hours.

Prepare the grill and cook the quail over medium heat for 5 minutes on each side. Let the quail sit for 3 minutes before serving.

BARBECUED SQUIRREL

- 4 small squirrels cut up
- 2–3 tablespoons olive oil
- 4 tablespoons spicy Chipotle rub
- 2 cups barbecue sauce
- 3 cloves garlic, minced
- 11/2 teaspoons toasted sesame oil

Rub the squirrel pieces with the olive oil and sprinkle with the Chipotle rub. Put the squirrel pieces in a single layer in a Dutch oven and set over the fire. Let the squirrel cook for 30 minutes.

Mix together the barbecue sauce, the garlic, and the sesame oil and pour it over the meat. Continue to cook for 60 minutes.

CHARCOAL GRILLED VENISON MEATLOAF

- 2 pounds ground venison
- 1 egg, beaten
- 1 onion, finely chopped
- 2 tablespoons brown sugar, optional
- 1/4 cup ketchup
- 1/2 cup cracker crumbs or bread crumbs
- 2 teaspoons prepared mustard
- Sauce:
- 1/4 cup ketchup
- 2 tablespoons brown sugar

- 2 teaspoons water

Mix together the venison, the onion, the ketchup, the brown sugar, the bread crumbs and the prepared mustard. Put this mixture into a metal loaf pan and place it on the grill. Let this cook for 15 minutes.

Combine the ketchup, the prepared mustard, the brown sugar, and the water. Remove the meatloaf from the pan and wrap it in some aluminum foil. Cover it with the sauce and continue to cook for another 10 minutes.

CHILI GRILLED WILD TURKEY KEBABS

- 1 tablespoon mild chili powder
- 1 small onion cut into chunks
- 3 garlic cloves
- 1 tablespoon fresh orange juice
- 1 tablespoon fresh lemon juice
- 1/4 teaspoon salt
- 1 teaspoon dried oregano
- 1 tablespoon vegetable oil
- 1 1/2 pounds of boneless wild turkey, cut into chunks

In a blender, combine the chili powder, the onion, the garlic, the juices, the salt, the oregano, and the oil. Process until it is minced and well blended.

In a bowl, mix together the chili powder mixture and the turkey. Marinate the turkey for 6 to 8 hours.
Place the turkey chunks on skewers and grill over hot coals for 3-4 minutes, turning occasionally until the chunks are cooked through

Photo by Haydn Blackey / CC BY-SA 2.0

- 2 rabbits, dressed
- 1/2 stick butter, melted
- 1/4 cup vegetable oil
- Juice of 1 lemon
- Barbecue sauce

In a large metal pot, place the rabbits with enough water to cover. Put the pot over a hot fire and bring it to a boil for 30 minutes. Remove the rabbit from the pot and drain. Put the rabbit on the hot grill, basting with the butter mixture, turning several times. Just before the meat is done, baste the meat with the barbecue sauce.

GRILLED DUCK

- 2 duck breasts
- 1 cup Italian salad dressing
- Salt and pepper
- 6 strips bacon
- 1 tomato, thinly sliced
- 1 onion, thinly sliced

Remove all of the skin and the fat from the duck. Put the meat in a bowl and mix it with the dressing. Let the duck marinate for at 30 minutes. Remove the meat from the marinade and season with the salt and the pepper. Cover the duck with the bacon strips and secure the bacon with toothpicks.

Put the duck on a foil lined baking sheet and place a tomato and onion slice on top of each breast.
Put the pan on the grill and cook 30 minutes. Then remove the duck from the baking sheet and place directly on the grill and cook 10 minutes longer.

GRILLED DUCK POPPERS

- 4 wild duck breasts
- 1 jar medium hot jalapeno pepper slices
- 1 pkg sliced uncooked bacon
- 1 pkg cream cheese
- 1 bottle Italian Dressing
- 1 box toothpicks

Place the breast in a plastic storage bag and pour the Italian dressing over the breasts. Let the duck marinate for 3-6 hours.

Remove the duck breasts from the marinade and cut them so there is an indent in the middle.
Place a slice of the cream cheese and several of the jalapeno peppers inside the cavity. Fold the breast back over so the cream cheese and the peppers are in the middle. Wrap the bacon around each breast and secure with toothpicks.

Place the breasts on the grill and cook for 5 minutes on each side. Serve each breast cut into small bite sized portions.

GRILLED VENISON BURGERS

- 1 1/2 pounds of ground venison
- 1 teaspoon of seasoned salt
- 2 teaspoons of Worcestershire sauce
- 1/4 teaspoon black pepper
- 2 tablespoons whipping cream

In a large bowl, sprinkle the meat with the salt, the Worcestershire sauce, the pepper, and cream. Blend the meat and the seasonings until they are evenly combined.

Shape the meat mixture into six burgers and grill 5 inches from the heat for 4 minutes on each side.

Photo by <u>Pa Van</u> / <u>CC BY 2.0</u>

- 1 8 to 10-pound boneless pork shoulder
- 1/3 cup lemon pepper seasoning
- 1 teaspoon salt
- 1 teaspoon black pepper
- 1 teaspoon paprika
- 1 teaspoon ground red pepper
- 1 teaspoon ground cumin
- 1 teaspoon chili powder
- Several handfuls of hickory chips

Let the hickory chips soak in water for 30 minutes. In a bowl, mix together the lemon pepper, the salt, the black pepper, the paprika, the red pepper, the cumin and the chili powder and rub the mixture evenly over the pork.

Add the hickory chips to the coals and put the pork on the grill. Cook the meat for 5 hours. Serve with your favorite barbeque sauce.

LEMON-GARLIC ELK STEAKS

Photo by Franco Folini / CC BY-SA 2.0

- 2 elk steaks
- 1/2 cup Italian dressing
- 2 tablespoons red wine, optional
- 1-2 cloves garlic, minced

Place the steaks in a shallow pan. Combine the Italian dressing, the red wine, and the garlic and pour over the steaks. Cover the meat and marinate for 24 hours. Place the steaks on a hot grill and cook each side for 8 minutes.

BARBECUED WILD TURKEY STRIPS

- Wild turkey breast, cut into 1/4 inch strips
- 1/2 cup soy sauce
- 1/2 cup water
- 2 tablespoons brown sugar
- 2 tablespoons olive oil
- 1/2 teaspoon crushed garlic
- 1/8 teaspoon black pepper
- 1 tablespoon lemon juice
- 1/4 teaspoon Tabasco sauce

In a bowl, mix together all of the ingredients and add the turkey strips. Marinate the meat for several hours and then drain, keeping the marinade. Place the turkey on a hot grill and cook for 10 minutes, basting often with the marinade.

GRILLED RATTLESNAKE

- 1 rattler per person
- 1/2 cup tomato chow chow
- 1 tablespoon chili powder
- 1 tablespoon oil
- 1 tablespoon molasses
- 2 tablespoon finely grated green pepper
- Salt and pepper to taste
- Juice of 1 lemon
- 2 tablespoon Worcestershire

Wash, dry and cut the snake into 4 inch pieces. Then, in a large bowl, mix all the ingredients and let the meat marinate for 2 hours. Arrange the snake on the hot grill and cook slowly, basting often. Serve when tender.

SWEET AND SOUR VENISON STEW

- 2 lb venison stew meat
- 1 can tomatoes
- 1/2 cup brown sugar
- 1/2 cup vinegar
- 1 onion, cut into pieces
- 1 green pepper, cut into pieces

In a large Dutch oven, brown the stew meat in the oil. Then add the onion and cook until the onion is tender. Add the mashed tomatoes, the vinegar, and the brown sugar. With just enough water so it
won't stick. Cook over an open fire for several hours until tender. Just before serving, add the green pepper strips.

BARBECUED RABBIT

- 1 rabbit
- 1 chopped onion
- Celery tops
- 2 tablespoons butter
- 1 garlic clove, chopped
- 1/2 cup chopped celery
- 3/4 cup water
- 1/4 cup dry wine
- 2 tablespoons vinegar

- 1 cup ketchup
- 2 tablespoons brown sugar
- 2 tablespoons Worcestershire sauce
- 1 teaspoon dry mustard
- 1 teaspoon salt
- 1/4 teaspoon pepper

Cut the rabbit into small serving pieces. In a Dutch oven, over hot coals, boil the rabbit with the celery tops for 30 minutes. Remove the rabbit from the water and let it sit for a few minutes. In the same pot, cook the onion in water until it has browned. Add the remaining ingredients and cook for 20 minutes. Add the rabbit back to the pot and simmer for 1 hour.

COUNTRY STYLE VENISON STEAKS

- 6 venison steaks
- Salt and pepper
- Charcoal seasoning
- Butter

One hour before grilling, sprinkle both sides of the steak with the salt, the pepper and the charcoal seasoning. Melt the butter in a large cast iron skillet over a hot fire. Cook the steaks for 3 to 5 minutes on each side. Serve while hot.

VENISON GOULASH

- 2 lb white onions, sliced
- 8 oz vegetable shortening
- 3 lb stewing venison, cubed
- 1 tablespoon margarine
- 1 1/2 tablespoons paprika
- 2 cans beef broth
- Noodles

In a large cast iron skillet, over hot flames, fry the onions in the shortening until soft. Add the venison and brown on all sides. Add the butter, the paprika, and the beef broth, cover pot and simmer 3 hours. Serve over cooked noodles.

RABBIT STEW

- Rabbit, cut into pieces
- 1 can tomatoes, mashed
- 1 onion, chopped
- Curry powder to taste

In a Dutch oven, brown the rabbit. Add the salt and pepper to taste. Mix together the tomatoes, the onions, the curry powder, the salt and the pepper and add to the browned rabbit pieces. Cook over an open flame for 3 hours.

PHEASANT AND MUSHROOMS

- 2 pheasants cut in serving pieces
- 1/2 cup pancake mix
- 1/2 cup margarine
- 2 cups mushrooms, sliced
- 1 onion, chopped
- 2 chicken bouillon cubes, dissolved in 1 cup hot water
- Juice of 1/2 lemon
- 1 teaspoon salt
- 1 teaspoon pepper

Roll the pheasant pieces in the pancake mix. In a cast iron skillet, brown the meat in the margarine. Remove the meat from the skillet and add the mushrooms and the onions and cook until brown.

Add the pheasant, the bouillon, the lemon juice and the seasonings. Cover the skillet and cook for 1 hour until tender.

PANNED DIAMOND RATTLERS

- 2 1/2 lb cleaned diamond back rattlesnakes
- 1/4 cup yellow cornmeal
- 1/4 cup cooking oil
- Salt and pepper

Salt and pepper the rattlesnake and roll the pieces in the cornmeal. In a large cast iron skillet, over hot flames, fry the snake until the pieces are brown on both sides. Serve with barbeque.

Photo by David Reber / CC BY-SA 2.0

- 2 lb frog legs
- 1 egg, beaten
- 1/2 cup cornmeal
- 1/2 teaspoon salt
- 1/8 teaspoon pepper
- 1/2 cup cooking oil

In a bowl, blend together the egg, the corn meal, the salt and the pepper to form a batter and batter the frog. In a cast iron skillet over hot flames, fry the frog legs in the oil for 25 minutes.

THANK YOU

If you have truly found value in my publication please take a minute and rate my book, I'd be eternally grateful if you left a review. As an independent author I rely on reviews for my livelihood and it gives me great pleasure to see my work is appreciated.